Investing Advice
For My Grandchildren

Leland M. Walker

LELAND M. WALKER

ISBN-10: 1539799239
ISBN-13: 978-1539799238

LELAND M. WALKER

DEDICATION

To Rusty (the dog)

LELAND M. WALKER

Contents

LELAND M. WALKER

ACKNOWLEDGMENTS

Thanks to my wife Pat for her help with proof reading and editing.

Thanks to Damion Anderson for his proof reading, suggestions, and encouragement.

This book contains images captured from E*Trade's web site. I use these images to help explain the use of their mutual fund screener.

This book contains a copy of a table from T. Rowe Price's web site which explains the differences between Roth IRAs and Traditional IRAs.

LELAND M. WALKER

1. Purpose

If you are reading this book I assume you are not wealthy and you would like to be. Or, you inherited some money and would like to know how to preserve and grow it. You may or may not be one of my grandchildren.

My Advice

If <u>any </u>of the following is true for you, then this book is not for you and you are wasting your time:

You have not finished your formal education.

You want to get rich quick.

You carry a balance on a credit card.

You drive a really nice car.

You are unable to provide the essentials for your family.

You don't pay your bills before the due date.

You have more than $1,000,000.

2. The Millionaire Next Door

The Steve Jobs and Bill Gates route to wealth is an unlikely way for you to achieve your goal. You probably have neighbors who are worth more than a million dollars and you don't know it. They probably drive a seven year old Toyota Camry to work every day. They accumulated their wealth by doing without and saving systematically. Most of the millionaires in this country became millionaires in this way.

My Advice

Get a liberal education (BA)

Get a job and keep it.

Don't get divorced.

Don't carry a balance on a credit card.

Don't drive an expensive car.

Manage to save something out of every paycheck.

3. Your Timeline

My Advice

Get a minimum of a Liberal Arts degree

Take one trip to a foreign country.

Decide on your career. Very likely you will need a graduate degree.

Go to work.

Begin to accumulate wealth.

Start your family.

In all cultures there are concepts about the "Stages of Life". They are all similar. They differ a little in the number of stages and the breakdown of what is in each stage, but basically they are all the same. In the Hindu culture it is called Ashrama. In this culture the properly lived life will not mix the stages or get them out of sequence.

The Ashrama System

Student Life	Till 24 years old
Household	24 to 48
Retired	48 to 72
Renounced Life	72 (or anytime after Student stage for a simple spiritual existence)

I lived my life with my stages mixed and out of sequence and this made things much more difficult than they could have been.

In our culture (American) we generally agree that a person should focus on getting a good education before settling down to a career and family. Most Americans also believe that the only time in your life it is acceptable to take money without earning it is when you are a student. You are allowed to beg, borrow, and accept gifts to get your degree. Focus that youthful energy and drive on getting your education.

Your education prepares you for the next stage of your life. Therefore, your education should prepare you for living, not just getting a job. However, education does open doors. With a limited education your options for a career are limited. With a liberal education your options are almost unlimited.

You should get a liberal education! I just can't say this enough. The only people who don't value a liberal education are the people who don't have one. Why do universities require you to take history, English, a foreign language, science, social studies, non-western thought, math, and sports? A liberal education gives you a broad base for making life decisions like what you want to do with your life. It also gives you the tools for being a critical, analytical thinker. You will be better qualified to vote intelligently. You will be a better parent and partner. You will be a better citizen. Your friendship will be valued. You will have a better life.

If you are out of phase, as I was, you can still get your education. I did, and it has made all the difference. If you are already working and have obligations, then it is even more urgent that you complete your education. Go nights. Go part time. Go on-line. But get it. It's just work! You do the work...you get the grade! This is the only life you are going to have. You need the knowledge, but also, you need those credentials!

4. Living within Your Means

Building wealth requires that you have some money left over out of each pay period, and it requires that you continue to live this way for 30 or 40 years. You have to be patient. You have to find your balance of enjoying the present and saving for the future.

My Advice

Getting a divorce is the most financially damaging thing you can do.

Carrying a balance on a credit card is the second.

Buying expensive cars is the third.

Fixing a car is almost always cheaper than trading.

This is going to be a very short chapter. Basically it is just "Don't spend more than you earn!".

It is simple arithmetic to determine whether you spend more than you earn. If you spend more than you earn, fix it. You need to earn more, or spend less, or both. And you need to do it right now!

About divorce...it will set you back financially 10 to 20 years. You never catch up.

The belief that you need a good credit rating is a vicious myth. This myth is just a trick to convince young people to borrow money. Don't buy into it. **Do not borrow money.**

Credit cards are very convenient only if you don't pay anything to use them. Pay off the balance every month and do not pay an annual fee. If you can't discipline yourself to do this, then you have no choice but to get the scissors and cut them up. Switch to a debit card. I know people who successfully took this step.

Car payments should be avoided if at all possible during the wealth building/family stage. When you finance a car you have the interest, but you also have to buy collision and comprehensive insurance that you don't need. If you have to finance a car make sure you use a bank and shop for a low interest rate. Our main street in Jonesboro is lined with Title Pawns and Pawn Shops. They prey on the ignorant and desperate. You are neither.

Home mortgages are good if you buy within your means and shop for best rates. Make sure you include the points and closing costs in your cost comparisons. Home ownership should be part of your wealth building and investing plan.

5. Investing Strategy

My Advice

Invest in good mutual funds.

Invest systematically

Invest for the long term (don't try to time the market)

Minimize the costs of investing.

Do it yourself.

Mutual Funds

A mutual fund is a legal entity that owns shares of stock in companies and other securities and holds cash. Mutual funds are created, held, and managed by brokerage firms such as T. Rowe Price, Fidelity, Charles Schwab, and E*Trade. There are others.

Selecting a broker is covered in Chapter 6.

Selecting "good" mutual funds is covered in Chapter 7.

You do not necessarily have to buy a mutual fund from the same firm that manages that fund. If you have an account with E*Trade they will sell you a T. Rowe Price fund, for example.

Some brokerage firms offer more types of services than others. For example, my Fidelity and E*Trade brokerage accounts have check writing and automatic money market deposit. But T. Rowe Price does not hold cash. They only hold shares of mutual funds. I will have more on this later.

You invest in a mutual fund by buying shares of the mutual fund. The value (price) of a share of a mutual fund is calculated each day after the stock market closes. The price is determined by taking the closing price of each of the stocks the fund owns and multiplying by the number of shares owned of that stock. They then sum the value of all the stock, plus cash, and divide the total by the number of outstanding shares of the mutual fund. The result is the price you pay for one share. When you invest cash in a mutual fund they divide the amount of your investment by the closing price of the mutual fund shares and create that many shares for you, down to a fraction (.001) of a share.

There exists another type of mutual fund. It is called an ETF

(Exchange Traded Fund). You will not invest in this type of fund. I only tell you about it so you will know to avoid it. The value (price) of a share of an ETF is determined only by what someone is willing to pay. ETFs are speculative and the values are more volatile. Volatility refers to how much the share price fluctuates day to day. We are not gamblers.

Invest systematically

Save regularly. Set up an automatic payment system so you won't have to think about it. Save the money before you see it.

When you buy your mutual funds you should buy a fixed amount of dollar's worth of shares on a fixed schedule. Here's why. The price of a share fluctuates. If the price is up you buy fewer shares. When the price is down you buy more shares. As a result, after a couple of years the average price you paid per share will be less than the average price.

Risk, Return, and Cost of investing

The reason for putting your money in Mutual funds is that it gives a small investor the diversification, low cost, and professional management that once was available only to the very large investors.

All investments have *risk.*

There is risk that the company you invest with or in might go broke. Then you lose some or all of your investment. Or, in the case of stock, the value of the stock might decline. Then you lose cash value of your investment. Of course you want risk to be small. Mutual fund investments are not federally insured (like bank deposits). So we are going to have to be very careful about selecting our mutual funds.

Generally, investments with a potential for large *returns* have a high *risk*. So you have to balance the risk with the return expected. For example, Federal bonds have a relatively low risk because if the Federal government runs out of money they can just print some more. But Federal bonds do not pay very much in returns. I do not recommend bonds or the Federal government. We can do better without significantly increasing risk.

Some people think they avoid risk completely by buying annuities. An annuity is where you give them your money and they promise to pay you a set amount per month for as long as you live beginning when you retire. The return on annuities is always negative, and you have no control of your money. **Never buy annuities**.

Conversely, investments in a small start-up company could result in enormous returns. For example, early employees of Winnebago became millionaires because they owned stock in the company. You can buy stock in small companies and you might get rich, but you will more likely lose your money. Most start-ups fail. I do not recommend investing in single companies.

Risk is reduced by *Diversification.*

In order to diversify you have to invest in a lot of companies. If you own a lot of different companies, 200 say, if one company goes broke you lose .5% of your investments. That is $500 out of a $100,000 portfolio. That wouldn't set you back very much. If all the companies you buy are financially sound you lower the risk. Mutual funds are diversified, and hopefully, the manager buys only financially sound companies.

Most investments have *returns*. Of course you want returns, else why invest? Returns are your earnings from your investment. Returns are the sum of dividends, interest, and the increase in the value of the shares. If you didn't get some return the value of your investment would decline in time due to inflation. Actually, you lose value if your rate of return does not exceed the rate of inflation. Every mutual fund prospectus states very clearly that past performance should not be taken as an indicator of future performance. Nevertheless, that is exactly what we do. We select funds that have historically performed well, and we fully expect future performance to be similar. Hopefully, the professional manager of our fund will continue to do the good job he has done for the past five to ten years.

We will invest in funds that invest in stock as opposed to those that hold bonds, cash, money markets, or annuities. The reason being, historically the stock market has always paid more return, even when you include the great depression. You are investing for the long term. The stock market is as secure as the U.S. economy.

There are *Costs* associated with investing.
Transaction fees are charged by brokerage firms for buying and selling securities. That is how they make their money. In the past, broker fees were more than they are now. You will buy your mutual funds on-line using a "discount broker". Discount brokers charge the same transaction fees for one share or for a hundred shares. Typically transaction fees are less than $10.00. There is one firm that charges only $5.00.

Diversification of individual stocks is costly. If you buy shares of stock in 200 companies you would have to conduct 400 transactions: 200 when you buy and 200 when you sell. Even with the most discounted broker with a transaction fee of $5.00 that would be $2,000! However, you will probably not pay any transaction fees at all. Read on.

Since you are buying a mutual fund, you only make one transaction. And, mutual fund transactions are usually free. In fact, we will try to buy only those with no transaction fees. Of course, mutual funds are already diversified, but you can diversify even more by buying two or three different funds.

Front-end Loads are charged by some mutual funds. If you invest $1,000 in a mutual fund with a 5% front-end load, $50 will pay for the sales charge, and $950 will be invested in the fund. You will not buy funds that charge a Front-end Load.

Back-end loads (also known as deferred sales charges) are very common. These are a bit more complicated. In such a fund you pay the back-end load if you sell a fund within a certain time frame. This is done to discourage you from trying to "play the market". For example, if you sell shares of a mutual fund less than 90 days from the day you bought shares of that mutual fund there might be a fee of $45. Most of the funds you buy will have this restriction, but it will not cost you anything because you will not buy a mutual fund if you think you might have to sell it within 90 days.

Expense ratio is the cost of managing the mutual fund. Management expenses cover administration expenses, managerial expenses, and profit for the brokerage firm that holds the fund. The fund is managed by a professional financial manager. These expenses are deducted from the fund and the cost is reflected in the share price. You will never pay any management expenses directly. You will minimize managerial expenses by buying only funds with a low (<1.0%) expense ratio. Typically, a large investor will pay a professional financial manager 1.0% of the value of his portfolio annually to manage his investments.

6. Opening a Brokerage Account

My advice

Select a discount broker.

Open one brokerage account.

Open one Roth IRA account.

Open one Roth IRA account for your spouse (if you have one).

Open additional accounts as appropriate.

The following link is to a list of discount Brokers provided by dogsofthedow.com.

http://www.dogsofthedow.com/tdbrokers.htm

If this list is no longer valid by the time you read this book you can ask Google for a similar list.

I have not used Scottrade, TD Ameritrade, nor TradeKing. I suppose they provide the same services as firms that I have used.

I have accounts with E*Trade, Fidelity, Charles Schwab, and T. Rowe Price. I am not recommending, endorsing, or commenting in any way on the pros or cons of any of these. These are merely the firms that I have used and I am familiar with how their web pages function. I will describe how to use these.

All this is done from your computer.

You will open a brokerage account by going to their web site and selecting the option for that purpose. You will be asked a lot of questions which you will answer based on your situation. For example, individual or joint account, retirement or investment, etc. I will not try to tell you how to answer all the questions that will be asked. I will tell you what kinds of accounts you should create.

You can open an account with no money.

You should use only discount brokers who do not charge anything unless you use them to buy shares of a security. Your brokerage account should be free. You will not incur transaction fees because you will not be buying stocks and you will select mutual funds that have no transaction fees.

T. Rowe Price does not hold cash.

Before you put money into a T. Rowe Price account you have to be prepared to tell them into which of their funds you want to put your money. This is not a bad thing. It just means you have to do Chapter 7 (How to Pick Mutual Funds) before you open an account with T. Rowe Price. If you want to invest in multiple mutual funds they will gladly distribute your investment equally over the multiple funds. You have to have enough cash for the minimum initial purchase. This is usually $2,500 or more for an investment account, and $1000 or more for an IRA (Individual Retirement Account) account. Once you own shares in a fund, subsequent minimum purchases are $100 or less.

Fidelity, Schwab, and E*Trade will accept your investment as cash. If you do not buy a mutual fund right away they will move your cash into a low risk, low yield deposit. The money earns a small, insignificant interest until you use it to buy shares in some security. When you accumulate enough cash for the minimum initial purchase you can buy shares in a mutual fund. Deposits (transfers into the account) are usually available immediately for investment, and available for withdrawal within three business days.

Some Brokerage accounts can be used like a bank.

Fidelity, Schwab, and E*Trade (and some others) have brokerage accounts that can be used as checking accounts. They offer all the conveniences of an on-line bank plus ease of buying and selling securities. I use my brokerage account for automatic bill pay, electronic bill pay, and automatic investment transfers to my IRA. The checking is free, they give you one book of checks free, and they pay a few cents interest each month. Fidelity refunds all ATM fees. Transfer capability between your bank and your brokerage account can be set up. Once you have this in place, you can transfer money back and forth at your computer.

You will find it convenient to have both a brokerage account and a Roth IRA (named for Senator William Roth) with your discount broker.

You will be asked whether you want a joint or individual brokerage account. IRA accounts are all individual.

You will be asked for beneficiaries for your accounts.

You will be asked what type of retirement account: Traditional IRA or Roth IRA. I am recommending Roth IRA. I copied the following table from T. Rowe Price's web site. You can study the differences and make up your own mind if you want. The basic difference is you pay the tax now or you pay it later. Since you are planning on being pretty rich when you retire you are not going to be in a lower tax bracket than you are now. So pay the tax now while your tax rate is low, and get all your earnings tax free. Taxes might go up, don't you think?

Roth IRA vs. Traditional IRA[1]

Roth IRA	Traditional IRA
Pay taxes now.	Pay taxes later.
Contributions may be withdrawn at any time without taxes or penalties.	**Contributions** may be tax-deductible.
Earnings may be withdrawn tax-free and penalty-free once you reach age 59½ and the account has been open for at least five years.	**Earnings** grow tax-deferred. You generally pay taxes when you make withdrawals, often in retirement.
No age restrictions for contributions.	You must be under age 70½ to contribute.
You may not be eligible to contribute if your income is $132k or more in tax year 2016 for single filers or $194k or more in tax year 2016 for joint filers.	No income restrictions on eligibility to contribute, but may be limit on deductibility.
No required minimum distributions (RMDs).	Must begin taking required minimum distributions (RMDs) at age 70½.

[1] This table is copied from T. Rowe Price's web site.

Maximum contribution for all IRAs is $5,500 per year per person ($6,500 if you are age 50 or over). After fully funding your IRA, if you still have money to invest buy mutual funds in your brokerage account.

When you buy shares in a mutual fund you will be asked what to do with the dividends and interest. You should pick "reinvest in fund". This is just a matter of convenience. You don't want it just sitting there not earning, and you don't want them to send it to you. Some funds pay dividends and interest once or twice a year.

7. How To Pick Mutual Funds

My advice

Learn to Select and purchase mutual funds.

Consider only funds with a 5 star Morningstar[2] rating.

Consider only no-load funds.

Consider only funds with expense ratio less than 1.0%.

Buy only Funds that have historically outperformed the market.

Buy Funds that invest in U.S. large or mid-cap stock.

Avoid Funds with short Management tenure.

---

[2] Morningstar is a leading market research and investment data group

Do not pay someone to select your mutual funds for you. Not only will they cut into your savings, but worse, they won't do a good job. Managed brokerage accounts tend to sell you their company's funds or funds from which they get a commission. In the worst case they will sell you an annuity, or, God forbid, they try to sell you insurance. They are biased and they have their own agenda. You have to do this yourself.

All of the brokerage web sites have tools for researching mutual funds. You will need to find and become familiar with a mutual fund screener tool on one of the brokerage sites. You might have to open an account to get access to their screener. You can open an account with most brokerage firms without a deposit.

I used the E*Trade mutual fund screener. I was logged into my account. I found the mutual fund screener under:

- Research

   - Products

      - Mutual Funds

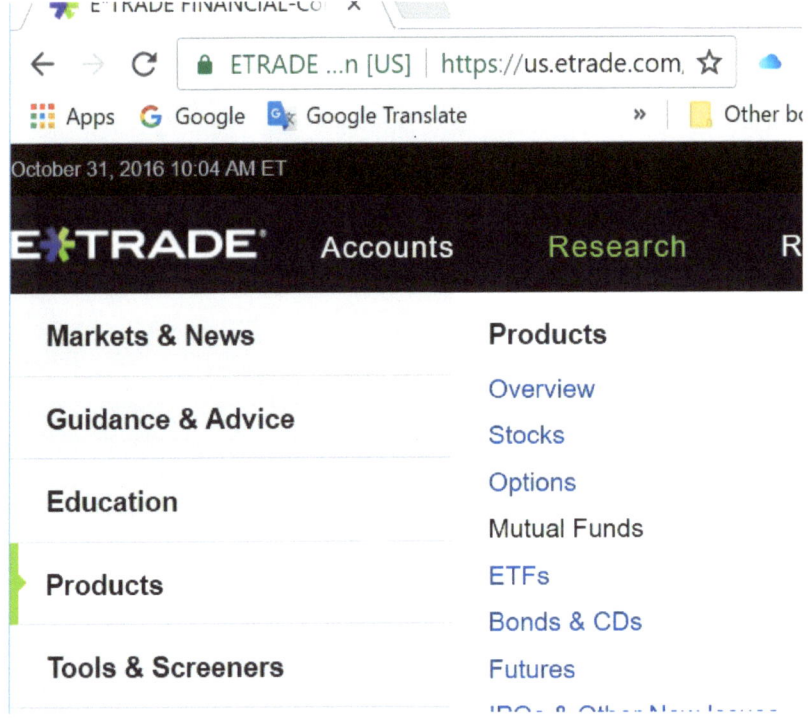

In the following example I searched using the following search criteria:

Category Group	Domestic Equity (U. S. Stock)
Fund Category	Large Growth
Morningstar Rating	5 Star
Open to New Investors	"Exclude funds closed to new investors"
Expense Ratio	Less than 1.0%
Fees	No Load No Transaction Fee

The search found four funds.

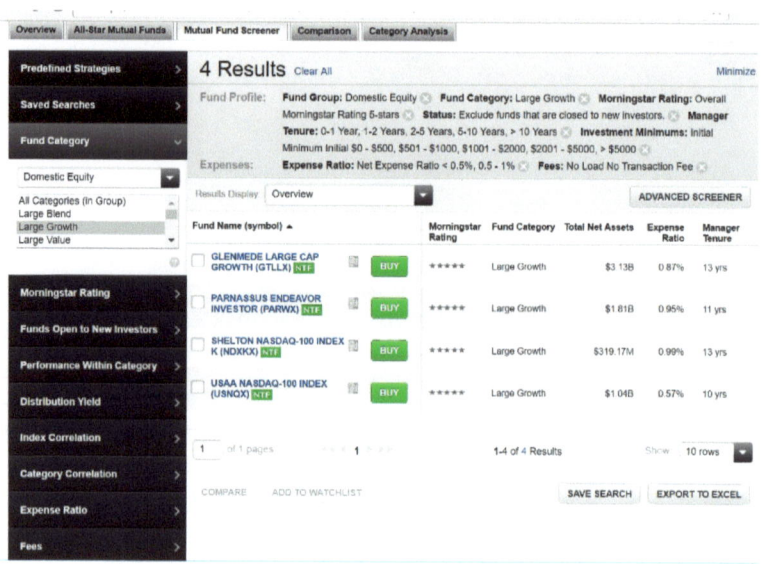

In this example I used the same criteria as before except I changed the category to "Large Blend". I obtained seven results.

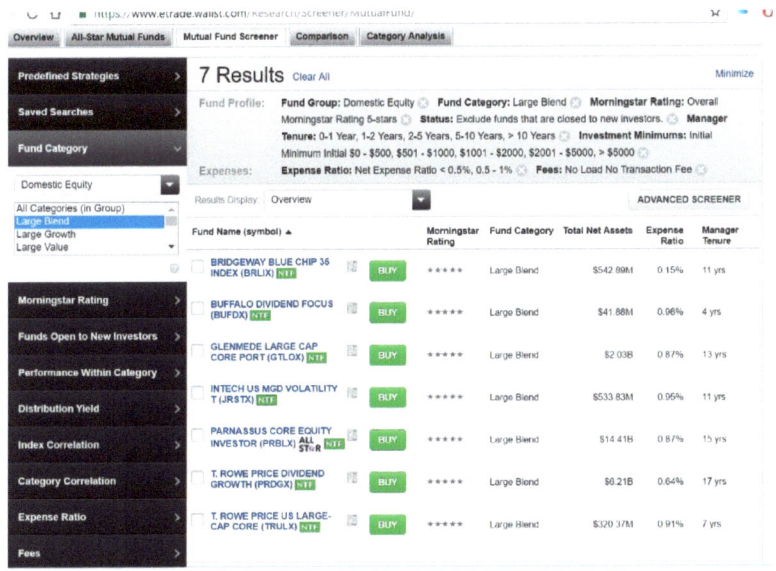

I now have a list of eleven mutual funds that are all

- Large U. S. stocks
- No load
- No transaction fee
- Five star Morningstar rating
- Open to new investors
- Less than 1.0 % expense ratio

Now we will take a look at the performance of these funds relative to the general market and to the category. There is a lot of good information on these charts. Take the time to study them.

Index funds are safe.

Let's just take the first one on "Large Blend" list and see how it goes. I click on the name of the fund and I get the following snapshot:

Net Asset Value	Today's Change	Public Offer Price	Previous Close	Trade
12.57	0.000 (0.00%)	12.57	12.57	BUY SELL

NASDAQ as of 10/27/16

📄 Fund Report 📑 Prospectus 📇 Add to Watchlist 📊 Historical Quote

Morningstar Rating as of 9/30/2016

★★★★★	Overall	1392 Funds
★★★★★	3 Year	1392 Funds
★★★★	5 Year	1210 Funds
★★★★★	10 Year	911 Funds

Category: Large Blend
Fund Characteristic: Index Fund

The investment seeks to provide a long-term total return on capital, primarily through capital appreciation, but also some income. The fund seeks to achieve its objective by approximating the total return of the Bridgeway Ultra-Large 35 Index (the "index"), a proprietary index composed by the Adviser, while minimizing the distribution of capital gains and minimizing costs. It normally invests at least 80% of its net assets (plus borrowings for investment purposes) in blue chip Company stocks included within the index. The fund invests in the stocks that comprise the index and seeks to approximately match the index composition and weighting.

Growth of $10,000

BRLIX
Large Blend
S&P 500 TR USD

BRLIX $20,358

$20,000
$17,500
$15,000
$12,500
$10,000
$7,500
$5,000
$2,500
$0

Manager John Montgomery's Tenure

2008 2009 2010 2011 2012 2013 2014 2015 2016

This graph represents the past growth of an investment of $10,000. The performance represented is past performance and is not intended to imply any future performance of the fund. It assumes reinvestment of dividends and capital gains, and does not reflect sales loads, redemption fees or the effects of taxes on any capital gains and/or distributions. The index is used for comparative purposes. Indexes are unmanaged and cannot be invested into directly.

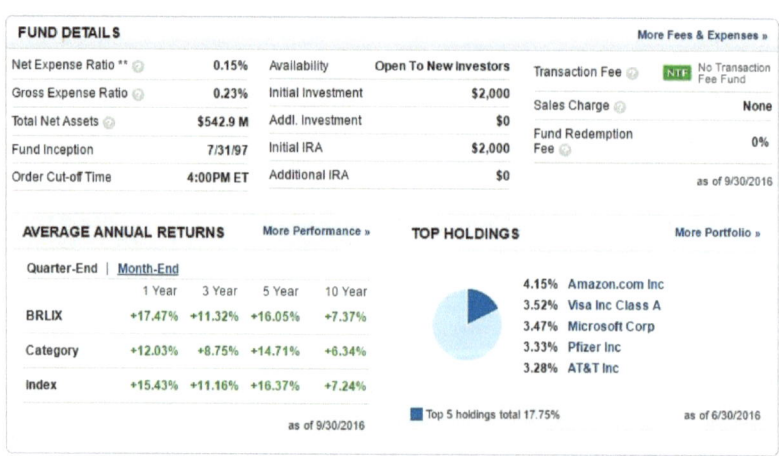

FUND DETAILS   More Fees & Expenses »

Net Expense Ratio **	0.15%	Availability	Open To New Investors	Transaction Fee	NTF	No Transaction Fee Fund
Gross Expense Ratio	0.23%	Initial Investment	$2,000	Sales Charge		None
Total Net Assets	$542.9 M	Addl. Investment	$0	Fund Redemption Fee		0%
Fund Inception	7/31/97	Initial IRA	$2,000			
Order Cut-off Time	4:00PM ET	Additional IRA	$0			as of 9/30/2016

AVERAGE ANNUAL RETURNS   More Performance »

Quarter-End | Month-End

	1 Year	3 Year	5 Year	10 Year
BRLIX	+17.47%	+11.32%	+16.05%	+7.37%
Category	+12.03%	+8.75%	+14.71%	+6.34%
Index	+15.43%	+11.16%	+16.37%	+7.24%

as of 9/30/2016

TOP HOLDINGS   More Portfolio »

4.15% Amazon.com Inc
3.52% Visa Inc Class A
3.47% Microsoft Corp
3.33% Pfizer Inc
3.28% AT&T Inc

■ Top 5 holdings total 17.75%   as of 6/30/2016

BRLIX has a very low expense ratio (0.15%). That is because it is an index fund. The stocks in this fund are purchased to match a particular index. For that reason there is very little work or research required in picking the stocks. Also, as an index fund the performance (growth, return) will match the market. You might like that because of the lower risk. Personally, I prefer mutual funds that outperform the market. I look for mutual funds that are more stable (less volatile) than the indicators, but increase in value more than the indicators over long periods. I look for funds that went up when the Dow Jones Industrial Average went up, but not as much. And, the fund went down when the Dow went down, but not as much. But, within a year's times the fund increased in value a little more than the Dow (or S&P 500, or NASDAQ).

To look at a performance graph and comparison graphs go to the "Charts" tab.

Let's take a look at PRDGX.

T. ROWE PRICE DIVIDEND GROWTH PRDGX
Fund Family: T. Rowe Price

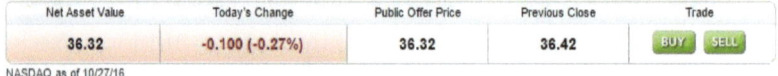

| Snapshot | Performance | Tax & Income | Risk & Ratings | Portfolio | Fees & Expenses | Charts |

Data quoted represents past performance. Past performance is not an indication of future results and mutual fund investment returns and share prices will fluctuate on a daily basis. Your investment may be worth more or less than your original cost when you redeem your shares. Current performance may be lower or higher than the performance data quoted. Unless specified, performance reflects the deduction of sales loads, adjustment for fund expenses, and reinvestment of dividends and capital gain. For most recent quarter end performance, select the Performance view.

**Certain funds may be subject to a cap on expenses or expense waiver. This fund does not have any expense caps, nor expense waivers.

Net Asset Value	Today's Change	Public Offer Price	Previous Close	Trade
36.32	-0.100 (-0.27%)	36.32	36.42	BUY SELL

NASDAQ as of 10/27/16

📄 Fund Report 📄 Prospectus 📄 Add to Watchlist 📄 Historical Quote

Morningstar Rating as of 9/30/2016

★★★★★	Overall	1392 Funds
★★★★★	3 Year	1392 Funds
★★★★	5 Year	1210 Funds
★★★★★	10 Year	911 Funds

Category: Large Blend
Fund Characteristic:

The investment seeks dividend income and long-term capital growth primarily through investments in stocks. The fund will normally invest at least 65% of its total assets in stocks, with an emphasis on stocks that have a strong track record of paying dividends or that are expected to increase their dividends over time. T. Rowe Price believes that a track record of dividend increases can be an excellent indicator of financial health and growth prospects, and that over the long term, income can contribute significantly to total return.

Growth of $10,000

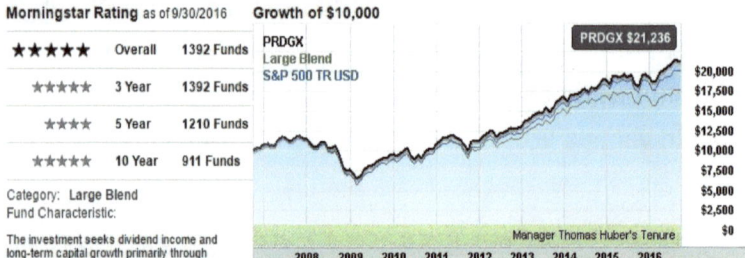

PRDGX $21,236

PRDGX
Large Blend
S&P 500 TR USD

This graph represents the past growth of an investment of $10,000. The performance represented is past performance and is not intended to imply any future performance of the fund. It assumes reinvestment of dividends and capital gains, and does not reflect sales loads, redemption fees or the effects of taxes on any capital gains and/or distributions. The index is used for comparative purposes. Indexes are unmanaged and cannot be invested into directly.

FUND DETAILS

More Fees & Expenses »

Net Expense Ratio **	0.64%	Availability	Open To New Investors	Transaction Fee	NTF No Transaction Fee Fund
Gross Expense Ratio	0.64%	Initial Investment	$2,500	Sales Charge	None
Total Net Assets	$6.2 B	Addl. Investment	$100	Fund Redemption Fee	0%
Fund Inception	12/30/92	Initial IRA	$1,000		
Order Cut-off Time	4:00PM ET	Additional IRA	$100		as of 9/30/2016

AVERAGE ANNUAL RETURNS

More Performance »

Quarter-End | Month-End

	1 Year	3 Year	5 Year	10 Year
PRDGX	+17.11%	+11.14%	+16.08%	+7.82%
Category	+12.03%	+8.75%	+14.71%	+6.34%
Index	+15.43%	+11.16%	+16.37%	+7.24%

as of 9/30/2016

TOP HOLDINGS

More Portfolio »

2.38% Microsoft Corp
2.34% Pfizer Inc
2.16% General Electric Co
2.01% Comcast Corp Class A
2.01% JPMorgan Chase & Co

■ Top 5 holdings total 10.89%   as of 9/30/2016

From these charts we see the expense ratio, initial investment, average returns, and top holdings for PRDGX.

The average returns look real good on an absolute level! 16% per year for 5 years is a really good average. The returns look good also when compared to the category average.

I would buy this fund. It meets all my criteria. But first I would look at the rest of the funds on our list to see if maybe there is something even better.

Dividends affect share price

Now look closely at these next two graphs. I want to point out how dividend distributions affect the share price of a mutual fund. This is the share price for PRDGX.

As I mentioned before, this graph is on the "Charts" tab. There you can select the time period and comparisons you want.

The first chart is YTD (year to date, January through October) comparison of the fund share price with the DOW and with the S&P 500.

The second chart is the same comparison except it is for a full year, ending October 27, 2016.

On the first graph PRDGX clearly outperforms both indices. On the second graph PRDGX does not perform as well as the indices. There is a simple explanation. The fund pays a dividend in mid December. When the dividend is paid the value of a share drops and the share holder gets an equivalent in cash or additional shares of the fund. This return in the form of a dividend is not reflected in the fund price, but it is reflected in the other chart which gives the average annual returns for 1, 3 or 5 years. Be aware of the effect of dividend payments when evaluating performance. Share price does not tell the whole story.

Secondary Considerations

Notice the other tabs at the top of the page. There is a lot of good information there. Here are some secondary considerations with which you will become familiar as you learn more about selecting mutual funds:

- Fund Prospectus
- Manager tenure
- Minimum investment
- The sector and types of securities
- The stated objective
- Diversification
- Turnover rate
- Risk/Return matrix
- Valuation/Size matrix

In conclusion, you now know all you need to know to start exploring the world of mutual funds.

My Advice

Find your balance between enjoying now and enjoying later.

Manage your finances.

Invest regularly.

Start early.

No fees.

ABOUT THE AUTHOR

Leland Walker lives in Jonesboro Georgia with his wife Pat, their dog Frank, and their cat Tuxedo. Leland has eleven grandchildren.

www.ingramcontent.com/pod-product-compliance
Lightning Source LLC
Chambersburg PA
CBHW040928180526
45159CB00002BA/660